Cage Your Rage for Teens

by

Murray Cullen and Joan Wright

ACA

FOUNDED 1870

American Correctional Association
4380 Forbes Boulevard
Lanham, MD 20706-4322

Copyright 1996 by the American Correctional Association

Bobbie L. Huskey, President
James A. Gondles, Jr., Executive Director
Gabriella Daley, Assistant Director, Publications and Communications
Alice Fins, Managing Editor
Michael H. Kelly, Associate Editor
Mike Selby, Production Editor

Inside Illustrations by Samuel T. Gibson, II
Cover by Graphic Mac, Inc., Washington, DC

Printed in the United States of America by Graphic Communications, Inc.,
     Upper Marlboro, MD

The reproduction, distribution, or inclusion in other publications or in electronic form of materials in this book is prohibited without prior written permission from the American Correctional Association. However, the Anger Logs and the Relaxation Logs may be reproduced.

ISBN 1-56991-036-7

This publication may be ordered from the:

American Correctional Association
4380 Forbes Boulevard
Lanham, MD 20706-4322
1-800-ACA-JOIN

Table of Contents

Acknowledgments

We formally acknowledge our spouses, who have put up with many lonely evenings while we have worked on this book. The staff members where Murray works have been very supportive of his efforts in the area of anger awareness, most notably Sandy, Marcella, and Marc. Thanks to Gil Rhodes for his support in treatment program efforts. Thanks and acknowledgments to Michael T. Bradley, my guide through the Ph.D. experience. Chris, Murray's four-year-old son, actually typed a few words of this manual, and we admit we needed his help to finish the project.

We formally acknowledge the dedicated staff who have worked with Joan to provide care and direction to troubled youth. This workbook would not have been possible without their invaluable input. The work of Dr. Eva Fiendler, an associate professor at Long Island University, New York, has proven to be a source of inspiration for Joan.

We direct you, the reader, to the workbook *Cage Your Rage* (also published by ACA) for a more detailed list of the many respected therapists, clinicians, and teachers, from whom we have learned so much in the area of understanding and treating people who experience problems with their emotions. For now, we will briefly mention them. Dr. Arthur Gordon first introduced Murray to this fascinating area and was generous with both his time and his information, including some of his unpublished manuscripts. Some of this information found its way into this book. Other useful information came from the work of Zender Katz. Many of the concepts in this book, such as the staging process, good and bad points about anger, as well as many of the management techniques come from Dr. Raymond Novaco's pioneering work.

We acknowledge the outstanding contributions of Dr. Albert Ellis for his work in the theory of emotions (including rational emotive therapy) and Dr. David Burns for his published works on cognitive distortions (thinking errors). Both of these come into play not only for the Cage Your Rage program but for nearly every anger management project. We have included other authors' works that provide useful information under "Suggested Readings."

Murray C. Cullen
Joan Wright

Foreword

Cage Your Rage for Teens augments the well-received Cage Your Rage program. We tested this material at several juvenile training schools and at a few public school sites. The result was a strong endorsement from both groups. We are pleased that we can now offer a program that will enable our young people to gain a tested method of curbing their rage and managing their problems with anger. We believe that an effective anger management program will slow the progression of many juveniles into a lifelong pattern of interaction with the criminal justice system.

For over 125 years, the American Correctional Association has been in the forefront of modern thinking about prisons, jails, and other correctional options. We are dedicated to stopping the growing upsurge in juvenile crime and in changing the way our leaders and fellow citizens view our ability to change people for the better. We know many things work. We believe this is one of the many positive programs which work.

We are interested in feedback from juvenile practitioners and other professionals who use this material. Please write us about the way that you use this material and what is particularly helpful in it. We also want to know what we should do to make this material more practical, so let us know its limitations for your use. Perhaps in revisions of it, we will be able to make this exciting and effective program even more useful.

James A. Gondles, Jr.
Executive Director
American Correctional Association

Introduction

Do you get angry?

Everyone gets angry from time to time. That is the way it always has been and the way it always will be. There is nothing wrong with being angry once in a while. In fact, it is quite normal. However, if you become overly aggressive when you are angry, you may hurt other people physically or verbally. At that point, angry feelings start to become a problem for you.

What type of book is this?

This is not just another book about angry feelings and aggression. It is much more than that. This book can help you learn about yourself: about your angry feelings and your harmful actions. It is a book about getting to know who you are and what you can do to become the person you would like to be.

Many people have lost control of their lives. They have lost control of their angry feelings. They hurt other people. However, they usually do not like being that way.

People who have problems with angry feelings and harmful actions often want to change. They want to have better control of themselves. They do not like to fly off the handle. They do not want to hit people. They do not like to cause trouble for other people. And, they do not like to get in trouble.

This book will help you get to know yourself. It will help you get to know how you think, how you got to be where you are right now, and how you can change your life. It will show you how to meet other people halfway and feel good about it.

How do I use this book?

This book is a workbook or journal. If you flip through the pages, you will find many personal questions that will make you think. You also will find spaces for your answers.

This is your book. It is your personal property, which you will be able to keep. Remember this so that you will feel free to write down your true feelings when you answer the questions.

What do I have to do?

It is important for you to decide that you want to change now. It is a big job, but you will not be alone. This book will help you.

What do you need to change your life?

You will need to accept yourself. You also will need the courage to admit that you have problems. It is hard to write about your faults. The easy solution is to run away from your problems. Yet, that will not help you change. To change, you must be honest with yourself. You must stay and face your problems. This book will help you.

Sometimes people keep their problems bottled up and do not say anything to anyone. They pretend their problems do not bother them. However, if they bottle up too many problems, they feel as if they have been hit with a sledgehammer. Have you ever felt that way?

It is very important to keep angry feelings from building up inside you. They will only hurt you. If you do not face them, you may hurt others when you do not mean to do so.

What is the bottom line?

This book is about how you get angry and how you get over it. It is about how you can get on with your life and feel much less angry and aggressive toward others. If you follow the program in this book, you will learn new ways to deal with your problems. Nevertheless, the biggest change must come from you!

You will need to read the book carefully and do the exercises. You may read this book all at once or a little at a time. Be sure you take time to do the exercises. If you put hard work and energy into this program, you can change your life.

Keep this book and reread it. After all, this book should become very important to you. It is about your life, your problems, and what you are doing to make positive changes. By answering the questions in this book, you will become the writer. You will write about a very special and important person in your life—you!

You are in charge

Experts agree that people get angry all by themselves. It may sound strange, but the truth is, no one can make you angry. Think about that. No one can make you hit someone or yell at someone. In fact, no one can make you feel anything at all. You are the one who decides how you feel!

Since you most likely learned to feel angry, you also can learn other ways to feel. You can learn to handle yourself in situations where you get angry. Some people have learned to be loud and violent in situations that make them angry. Others have learned to be kind and gentle in the same types of situations. You, too, can learn to leave most violence behind you. There is an alternative to loudness and violence—a way that will not make you feel bad or make others feel bad. You can learn how!

1 Anger Past and Present

What is anger?

Anger is a human emotion similar to joy or sadness. Many teens do not choose to get angry. However, when they are angry, they deal with their anger by keeping it from building up. Others keep their anger bottled up inside. Maybe they do not know how to deal with anger, or maybe they choose not to deal with it. They just ignore it. Yet, anger does not just go away. It can numb you so you do not feel it. It stays with you and causes ulcers, headaches, or sore muscles. You could say that bottling up angry feelings is a way of being violent to yourself, a way of causing yourself pain.

Does this happen to you?

You are angry, but you refuse to admit it. You keep your anger bottled up inside. As a result, you may act cold or stubborn to other people. You may stop hanging around with certain people. You arrive late for a class or an appointment—on purpose.

Or, do you let your anger grow until you explode? You lose control, scream, kick, throw things, punch or even stab someone.

The sad part is that both the victim and the attacker usually feel sorry later. Often the attacker has overreacted. The victim may have been at the wrong place at the wrong time. It is often the case that the attacker and the victim are close friends. The attacker may feel truly sorry. Attackers may feel that they had no other choice and simply lost control. They had so much anger bottled up that almost anything could make them blow their top.

Do not keep your angry feelings bottled up inside. They will only cause you problems and pain.

Do you belong to this group?

Some people let other people pull their strings—just like someone pulling the strings of a puppet. This happens quite often in school. Students get to know another student's pattern of acting and know just what strings to pull to set off the victim. For example, it might get you quite angry if another teen says to you, "Hey, while you were out playing soccer the other night, I saw your girlfriend with another guy; they were at the mall—necking."

That troublemaker knows exactly what to say to make you angry. He or she even may know what you will do when you get angry. People like that are controlling you! They are controlling your anger, which is controlling you. They know how to pull your strings.

There is hope. Do not go and do something stupid that you would regret later. Besides, there may be a hundred others just like these people, waiting to pull your strings. The answer is to pull those strings back up inside you. Get them out of sight. Doing that will help you get more in control of your life. That is the whole idea of this book—to get you to pull your own strings!

Growing up with anger

You have already taken a giant step toward change. You have agreed to read this book.

The second step will be harder. You will have to answer a number of questions. You must be truthful with yourself about your answers. The questions may bring back many memories of your early life, some good and some bad. Some memories may be sad. Yet, it is very important that you write your answers down on paper. Once they are written down, you can start to deal with them.

You may not realize it, but your past problems may be influencing your present actions, thoughts, and feelings. Imagine walking into an unfamiliar room at night with the lights out. It would be hard to find your way because you would not know what was in front of you. It is always best to turn the lights on to see. It is the same with the exercises in this book. They will be the lights that will help you see some of the problem areas in your past.

Most likely, you will have a lot of feelings—both good and bad—while doing the exercises. You may feel very sad, hopeless, and sometimes even unloved. Do not worry. These feelings will pass.

It is important for you to be alone in a quiet place when you answer the questions. Maybe the best place is your bedroom—if you have one. There, other people will not be as likely to interrupt what you are doing. If you have a stereo, you might want to listen to some music on the headphones. Whatever quiet spot you can locate, be sure to find a place where you will not be disturbed.

You may find the exercises very difficult. That may be because you will be answering the questions alone—without help from your parents, brothers, sisters, or anyone else. You will have to describe how you felt in the past. You will have to write about things that your family said or did to you. No one will be there to support you. Instead, you will have to think about how you felt then and how you feel now. Doing this takes a lot of courage. Be honest with yourself. It is a very big step, but you are doing it for yourself!

Think back to when you were a child and started to have ideas of your own. You listened to other people and tried to develop your own beliefs or opinions. You admired some people and did just what they did because it seemed right. You were very much affected by other people. You were like a ball of clay that other people were shaping into their idea of what was right. They may have forced their ideas on you. You were just a young child, and you needed those people. You thought that everything they did was right or for the right reasons. You never thought that maybe some of the adults and other children were mixed up. You were trying to find out who you were and what was right and what was wrong.

Now, we turn to the other side. Many parents only want to do what is right for their children. Most parents love their children very much. Even if they do what they think is right, it sometimes has bad effects on the child. For example, some parents think that the best way to teach children right from wrong is to slap or spank when the children do something wrong. These parents are teaching the child that it is okay to hit other people if they think it is for the right reason.

In many cases, children know that they have done something wrong. They may promise not to do it again, but the parents do not listen. They really do not hear the child. Instead, they use force and end up teaching the wrong lesson.

In many ways, these parents are like little children. They need someone to help them, to teach them the right way to do things. They need to learn a better way to cope with life. In many instances, the parents do not pay attention to children. They ignore the children's needs to satisfy their own needs. What message do children get from being ignored? The message might be—I do not love you, and I do not care about you. You are not important enough for me to care about you. I am your parent and should be the one person most concerned about you, but I am not. You are a worthless person and not worth my time.

These types of messages often have bad, long-lasting effects on children. Many teenagers think of themselves as worthless, unloved, and rejected. It is sad that many parents treat their children the same way that they were treated when they were children. They may be thinking, it worked for me, so it will work for them. I made it through and so can they! Yet, it does not have to be that way. There is another way to live.

A little care and understanding can go a long way to ease bitter feelings or angry situations. Care and understanding can lead the way to new and stronger relationships.

One of the major goals in this program is to get you to look back on events that happened in your life. Have you had a rough life? Have people been mean to you? If they have, you can learn to live with it. You really do not have to carry around all that baggage of hurts from the past. In your own mind, you can go back to those persons, even to family members, and try to understand why they treated you the way they did. Maybe you can talk to them and try to work out your differences. You might be surprised to find that they have a lot of anger, hurt, and even guilt from those past years.

Here are some questions. Use them to start exploring your past and your hurt feelings. Start from when you were a child. Try to remember how you felt at the time. Be honest about how you feel now.

ANGER QUESTIONS

PART I: Growing up with anger

1. Your folks

A. Who looks after you? Who is raising you? (parents, step-parents, group home staff, institutional staff)

_____

_____

_____

B. Describe the people who look after you now.

_____

_____

_____

2. Quality time

A. How do the people who look after you get along with each other? (Do they laugh and enjoy each other's company, or do they argue?)

_____

_____

_____

_____

B. How do they get along with you, now?

_____

_____

_____

_____

C. Do they spend a lot of good, quality time with you? Do they pay attention to you, or do they ignore you?

_____

_____

_____

_____

3. How your folks act

A. What happened when you did something wrong as a child? (Did someone scold you, discipline you, spank you, or hit you? Were you punished in some other way?)

_____

_____

_____

_____

_____

B. Did you think that your family was any different from anyone else's family at the time? (Think about what happened when you did something wrong as a child.)

_____

_____

_____

_____

_____

C. How is your family different from or the same as other families?

_____

_____

_____

_____

4. Run-ins with the law

Do the people who look after you ever have run-ins with the law? (If they do, please describe those run-ins. How often do they happen?)

_____

_____

_____

_____

_____

5. How your folks punish the family

A. How do the people who look after you punish other members of your family (brothers or sisters)?

_____

_____

_____

_____

_____

_____

B. How do the people who look after you punish each other?

_____

_____

_____

_____

_____

C. Do the people who look after you like your neighbors? Why do you think they feel that way?

_____

_____

_____

_____

6. Good times and bad times

A. How do the people who look after you deal with the good times?

_____

_____

_____

_____

B. How do they deal with the bad times? (Do they drink or use drugs? Are they violent?)

_____

_____

_____

_____

7. Growing up

How did it feel to grow up in your family?

_____

_____

_____

_____

8. Angry feelings

A. What is the anger like in your home? What were your first exposures to anger? How does your family express anger?

_____

_____

_____

_____

B. What happens when you become angry? (What do you do, and how do other family members react?)

_____

_____

_____

_____

_____

C. Is there usually an angry person around at any given time?

_____

_____

_____

_____

D. Are there any family members (or other adults) who are never angry? If so, how do you relate to them?

_____

_____

_____

_____

_____

E. How much of a problem do you think you have with anger? Does it interfere with your relationship with your friends, parents, teachers, boyfriends, or girlfriends?

_____

_____

_____

_____

_____

_____

_____

_____

_____

_____

_____

_____

F. How is your anger likely to get you in trouble?

_____

_____

_____

_____

_____

_____

_____

_____

_____

_____

_____

_____

_____

_____

G. How do you think that learning to control your anger will make your life different?

_____

_____

_____

_____

_____

_____

_____

_____

_____

_____

_____

_____

_____

_____

_____

9. Hate

A. Do you ever hate people in your family? If so, please explain why you hate them.

_____

_____

_____

_____

_____

B. Do they or did they know you hate them? How do they feel toward you?

_____

_____

_____

_____

_____

10. Drinking and drugs

A. Does anyone in your family have a drinking or drug problem?

_____

_____

_____

B. How does the person with the drinking or drug problem act? Does that person hurt you or others in the family? How?

_____

_____

_____

_____

_____

11. Early abuse

A. Did anyone ever abuse you physically or sexually as a child?

_____

_____

_____

B. If so, describe how you felt (angry, hurt, unloved).

_____

_____

_____

_____

C. How do you now feel about being hurt in the past?

_____

_____

_____

_____

12. School

In school, are you ever picked on by teachers or other students (either verbally or physically)? Please explain how you felt about it then and how you feel about it now.

_____

_____

_____

13. Your family

Do you think that the members of your family truly care for you? Please explain.

_____

_____

_____

_____

14. Your friends

A. Describe your close friends.

_____

_____

_____

_____

_____

_____

B. Do you ever talk to your friends about their families? Do you talk about how your friends are punished or if they are hit? How about drinking and drugs in their families? Please explain.

_____

_____

_____

_____

_____

_____

15. Help when things go bad

A. If things are bad at home, is there a place you can go? (church, recreation center, relative's house, friend's house) Please explain.

_____

_____

_____

_____

_____

_____

B. Are there other grownups or other teens who like you, even if you think your parents do not like you? Please explain.

_____

_____

_____

_____

_____

_____

_____

16. Summary of childhood

A. Write about your childhood: how you felt and what happened to you.

_____

_____

_____

_____

_____

_____

_____

_____

_____

_____

_____

_____

_____

_____

_____

_____

17. Present relationships

Does the way you were treated when you were younger affect how you treat others now? In what ways?

_____

_____

_____

_____

_____

_____

_____

_____

_____

_____

18. Instrumental aggression

There are two types of aggression: instrumental aggression and hostile aggression. Hostile aggression means that you hit and hurt someone. Instrumental aggression means that you attack someone to get something from them. An example of this is a bully in the school yard who knocks down a little girl to get her ball. The bully probably does not hate the girl, he just wants to get the ball. He thinks, if I come on strong and use a show of force, I'll get what I want.

A. Do you use instrumental aggression? How?

_____

_____

_____

_____

_____

_____

_____

_____

_____

_____

_____

_____

_____

_____

_____

B. Does anyone in your family use instrumental aggression? How do they use it?

_____

_____

_____

_____

_____

_____

C. Does anyone close to you (friends, teammates, girl/boyfriends) use instrumental aggression? How do they use it?

_____

_____

_____

_____

_____

_____

_____

_____

2 Anger and Aggression

Anger and aggression may seem hard to understand. Yet, you should know how anger and aggression work so you can control them.

Anger is a feeling like joy or sadness. When something bothers us, we can ignore it or we can get angry. When we get angry, we lose our patience. Our blood pressure goes up. We feel hyper and may not control what we say or do. We may throw things, break things, hit people, or curse them. That type of behavior is called "aggression." If we do not deal with our feelings of anger, they often lead to aggression. We may end up hurting someone.

Good points about anger

Anger has good points and bad points. Here are four of its good points:

1. Anger gives us energy. If we are in danger, anger gives us extra energy. It gives us a lift when we need it.
2. Anger helps us talk with others. Anger helps us talk about our bad feelings. That helps keep tension from building up inside of us.
3. Anger gives us information. When we feel angry, we should try to stop and think why we are angry. Something may be happening that is making us feel tense or uptight. Our anger could be a hint that something is making us feel stress.
4. Anger gives us a feeling of being in charge. Sometimes anger makes us feel we are in control. It feels good to be in control of situations and ourselves.

Bad points about anger

Anger also does bad things to us. Here are four of its bad points:

1. Anger stops us from thinking, feeling, and acting clearly. When we are very angry, we see red and find it hard to think clearly. This stops us from finding better ways to act. We end up doing something before we think about it.
2. We become angry much more often than we have to. We use anger to defend ourselves when we do not need to do so. For example, when we are embarrassed, we may become angry because it is easier to be angry than to feel embarrassed. It is easier to hurt others than to have our pride hurt.
3. Anger and aggression are related to each other. We may be angry for a long time. We may become angry very often. In those cases, we become aggressive. When we become aggressive, we say or do things that hurt others.
4. When we become angry, people think about us differently. We have learned about instrumental aggression. Remember the school bully who is not really angry at the little girl, he just wanted to get the ball she had? He may feel that this type of behavior makes him a tough guy. Some people may see him as a tough guy, but others may think of him as a jerk. No one really likes him. If he hangs around you, it is for the wrong reasons. It is not because he enjoys being with you. He is not really interested in you and is not a true friend. Think about it. Would you really want to hang around someone who does not care about anyone else? He could turn on you at the drop of a hat. He might hurt you for no real reason. Would you want to hang around that type of person?

Remember, anger is simply a feeling. Everyone has feelings of anger from time to time. However, aggression hurts people. If you can learn to deal with your angry feelings, then your anger will not lead to aggression. You can use your anger for all the good aspects listed. You can learn to stay away from the bad parts of anger. If you can do that, you will get along much better with your friends and your family.

How to stop your angry feelings from becoming a problem

1. **Avoid having angry feelings too often.**
   During a week, there are times when you may have a right to be angry. Suppose you know that another student stole something from your locker. That is good cause for anger.

Yet, there are also many times during a week when you do not need to have angry feelings. If there is no real reason to get angry, you just end up feeling uptight and hyper for nothing. Try to stop yourself from becoming angry easily. If you do not know all the facts, there is no need for you to rage at someone. Try not to second guess what another person is saying or doing to you. Find out the facts *before* you explode!

Many teenagers say, "Yeah, that sounds good, but it is not that easy. You either have to fight or be called a 'wimp.'" There are other choices. There are some teens, though, who say that you do not have to play the "tough person" role.

You can keep your angry feelings from becoming a problem by controlling the times when you are angry. Try to keep down the number of times that you get angry or bent out of shape when it is not necessary.

2. **Avoid having your anger become too strong.**
   Sometimes, anger is stronger than at other times. For example, someone accidentally spilling your can of Coke is far different from someone stealing from your locker. A nasty remark from a teacher is different from your boyfriend or girlfriend seeing someone else.

When your anger becomes very strong, you may start to feel the bad points described here. You will think less clearly, and you may be more easily enraged. There is a good chance that you will act before you think.

You can stop anger from becoming a problem by keeping the level of your anger down. When you are very angry, you put a lot of stress on your body. Keeping the level of your anger down can help reduce the wear and tear on your body. It also may give you more energy to do the things that you enjoy.

3. **Avoid being angry for long periods of time.**
   The stress on your body is worse if you are angry for a long time. Your body does not get a chance to gear down and return to normal. That makes you feel even worse and more easily upset. You may end up keeping yourself angry. You might do this by remembering all the times that you were upset in the past. For example, you may remember the time when you were criticized in front of your friends or when you were disciplined after coming in fifteen minutes past your curfew.

Many teenagers complain that they are unfairly treated by parents and teachers. It often seems that you are singled out for doing something wrong when all you were doing was minding your own business. If that sort of experience happens to a teenager once or twice, it is much easier to get angry at the teacher or parent when little things happen. It is best to deal with feelings of anger when they start. That way, anger does not have a chance to build up, and when you do get angry, the angry feelings will be less strong and much shorter.

4. **Do not let anger drag on until it becomes aggression.**
   As we have seen before, anger can lead to aggression—hostile or injurious behavior. That usually happens when angry feelings last too long or happen too often. When you are angry, it is important to ask, "Is it really worth it?"

Try to imagine the following scene. Four of you are in your living room arguing about the World Series. You get into a shouting match with a fellow who is about your size. Your muscles tense, your voice gets louder, you lean forward, shake your fists, and stare at him. At times like this, there is a good chance that you might strike out at him. You are becoming a problem for the other guy because you are cornering him.

What is he supposed to think of how you are acting toward him? He probably thinks that you are getting ready to hit him. He might consider hitting you first. What started as a simple disagreement over a baseball game may end up becoming a fight.

We talked about anger leading to aggression. This does not always mean that when you get angry, you hurt another person. In fact, the other person might get angry and hurt you! Getting into arguments or fights is a poor way of handling your bad feelings. For one thing, either you or the other person could get hurt. Further, you might lose out on good-time because of the event.

It is much better to "think before you leap." Find a better way to handle the problem. You might be thinking, that is easy for you to say. However, problems can be resolved—regardless of the situation. Teenagers have worked out their differences. It is possible!

5. **Do not let your anger interfere with your day.**
   Do not let it interfere in your relationships with other people. Imagine having a fight with your mother early in the morning. Think of what frame of mind that would put you in when you got to school. You may be very irritable with other people, including your teachers. You may do a lousy job on your schoolwork.

In another example, you are walking the hallway at school, minding your own business, when someone comes rushing past and knocks you against the wall, spilling your books and papers on the floor. You catch up with him, and a cursing match starts. Even though the principal did not catch you, you go through the rest of the day feeling uneasy and apprehensive. You might be afraid that the other teen might try to get back at you. The teachers might find out, and you might get a detention or be expelled. You still might be steaming about the whole issue.

All of these problems might be even worse. The other student may be in the same classes as you. Because of the unresolved problem, you have a lousy day. You might keep looking over your shoulder out of fear. You might be planning how to get back at the other teenager. Then, later that day you have a date. You are short-tempered with your date. Your date is having a tough time and wants your support. Instead, you only make wisecrack answers. You criticize your date, and you are rude to this person who cares for you.

Now, it might be true that you love this friend very much. You are, in fact, very glad that he or she made the trip to see you. Yet, right now, you are not in the right frame of mind to see anyone. That is because you have a problem that you have not dealt with—the other student in the hallway. You even might think, because of that clown I am having a lousy time with my date. I'll have to get that _____ back! Again, angry feelings lead to aggression later.

You have to keep angry feelings from getting in the way of your schoolwork and your relationships. They will keep you from feeling satisfied with school and your relationships with other people. As this example shows, your angry feelings might push other people away from you. They might make it difficult for other people to like you.

In summary, you can work at keeping anger from becoming a problem for you in the following ways.
1. Try not to have angry feelings too often.
2. Try not to experience angry feelings too strongly.
3. Try to get over your angry feelings quickly.
4. Work at making sure your angry feelings do not lead to aggressive acts.
5. Do not allow angry feelings to get in the way of your work or your relationships with other people.

Simply reading the previous section should help you to understand how anger can mess up your life. You can choose another option. Anger does not have to defeat you. This is an important step in preventing it from happening.

ANGER QUESTIONS

PART II: What happens when you get angry?

We have considered what anger is and how we can prevent it from becoming a problem. Now, we will put the focus back on you. Here is another set of questions for you to answer.

When you answer them, choose a quiet place away from other people. Be ready to think deeply and honestly about yourself and your angry feelings. Once again, swallow hard and have the courage to answer these questions truthfully.

1. Think about the time in your life when you were the most angry. How did your body feel? (Examples: hot, sweaty, tight-chested, filled with tension in your neck and shoulders)

_____

_____

_____

_____

_____

_____

_____

_____

2. Often your body will give you clues that you are becoming angry. Perhaps before you even realize that you are getting angry, your heart will beat faster or your skin will feel cold and clammy. Your thoughts might start to cloud. In your case, how do you usually feel when you get angry?

_____

_____

_____

_____

_____

_____

3. How often do you become angry? (How many times each day or each week?)

_____

_____

_____

4. What happened the last time you got angry? What did you feel and what were the clues that your body gave you? What did you say or do? How did the other person react? How was the problem resolved?

_____

_____

_____

_____

5. A. Do you sometimes wake up feeling angry?

_____

_____

_____

_____

B. When you do wake up feeling angry, do other people easily get you going? Give some examples.

_____

_____

_____

_____

_____

6. In general, how do you feel about your anger? (For example, do you usually think you have a right to be angry? Is your anger sometimes out of control?)

_____

_____

_____

_____

_____

7. Do you have control over your anger?

    A. Do you feel that your anger controls you?

_____

_____

_____

_____

    B. Do you ever feel crazy when you are angry? Please explain.

_____

_____

_____

_____

8. Describe a person or a situation that you reacted to by becoming angry recently.

_____

_____

_____

_____

_____

9. Have you ever been angry at yourself? (For example, were you angry because of the way you look, the way you act, where you are, the way your life is going, or the way you think?) Please explain.

_____

_____

_____

_____

_____

_____

10. What is the worst thing that you ever did when you were angry?

_____

_____

_____

_____

Pat yourself on the back. Answering these questions took a lot of time. It may have been very hard for you. Take a break.

③ What Causes Anger?

You are doing great! It was hard to answer some of the questions in the last section.

So far, we have talked about what anger is and what you can do to keep angry feelings from becoming a big problem for you. You have answered many questions about yourself. Those questions and answers have helped you learn more about your own anger. Now, let us examine what causes anger.

Millions of people in the world get angry for many different reasons. We can break down the reasons why most people get angry into two groups—outside reasons and inside reasons.

Outside reasons are those situations outside of you, which you react to by feeling angry. They are situations over which you have no control. Here are some examples of outside reasons that may make you angry: you are pushed in the food line or are called names by other teens, or you are punished for something that you did not do.

Inside reasons have to do with how you think and feel. They are a combination of outside and inside reasons—what you do as a result of a situation.

Outside reasons

Something that happens that is beyond your control is an outside reason. There are four different types of outside reasons.

1. Frustrations

You may feel frustrated when you are kept from doing something that you want to do. You may feel frustrated when you are unhappy with the results of something you did. One example of frustration is failing a test that you worked very hard to pass. Another example is having to get from one place to another and having to wait for a parent to take you. When you become frustrated, you may become jumpy, and you may become angry.

2. **Annoyances and irritations**

These are things that get on your nerves. It may be a student who is always annoying you or a teacher who always seems to be riding you. Irritations might include noisy people who blare their music or those who do not care about others. Annoyances might be people who are always interrupting. Sometimes, you might feel irritated just watching another person irritating someone else. Even breaking a guitar string might bother you.

3. **Abuse**

There are two types of abuse—verbal and physical. Verbal abuse includes: name calling, cursing, making sarcastic comments, and making other nasty or hurtful comments. Physical abuse includes: pushing, shoving, grabbing, punching, kicking, or inappropriate sexual situations. You may have had both types of abuse happen to you from time to time.

4. **Injustice and unfairness**

This occurs when you feel that you were not treated fairly. Teenagers often complain about being treated unfairly in school and at home. They often think that they are considered guilty and never have a chance to give their side of the story. You may feel angry when you see others, such as family or friends, treated unjustly or unfairly.

Inside reasons

These are the head games that you play on yourself. Most experts think that you "learned" to be angry or aggressive toward other people. Remember, when you get angry, you get angry all by yourself! Although it sounds funny, no one can make you angry. No one can make you hit or yell. You are the only person who makes the decisions. You decide how you feel, think, or react to things that bother you.

Here is how five different people might react to the same situation:

The situation: A teenager goes to get his pay for the last two weeks from his part-time job. His paycheck is shortchanged by five hours!

Depending on how your day is going, the mood you are in, or your attitude towards another person, you will react differently towards him or her—maybe in an angry manner. If you are having a string of bad luck, maybe you are looking for someone to blame or someone on whom to unload. Or, perhaps you can see that it was an honest mistake and you are able to keep your cool. We will see how five people dealt with the same situation.

1. He may have some bad feelings about the assistant manager who is handing out the paychecks. He might feel that person is giving him a hard time. He might think that the assistant manager ripped him off on purpose so he would quit and the manager could hire somebody he liked better. He might think that this is another bad experience he is having that day. He may explode into a rage and curse and swear at

everyone around him for the rest of the day—that is, until he swears at the wrong person who mops up the floor with him.

2. Another teenager may put the blame on the person who calculates the hours. He may think, that ___, I'll get him. He thinks that he can do whatever he wants. He can mess around with me, and there is not a thing I can do about it, but I'll show him. I'll get the money if I have to steal it! This type of thinking could result in a big argument with the accountant. It could result in the teenager losing his job and being charged with uttering threats, or even worse, a robbery conviction.

3. For another teen, the loss of pay may mean that he will come up short paying his bills. He may start to panic and think, now what am I going to do? I owe my friend money, and if I do not pay him back on time, he may not trust me again or worse, he may not believe me when I tell him that I was not paid my full wages. He may not speak to me and may try to start a fight or get others to beat me up.

4. Still another teenager may think that the accountant must have made a mistake in calculating his pay, again. This is the third time that it happened, and he thinks, I am really starting to get upset. I have to try to keep my cool, or I will make the situation worse. I will ask the assistant manager to look into it for me. I am worried about not being able to pay my bills on time, but I am sure my friend will understand. I will pay him most of what I owe him and go short myself.

5. A fifth teen may start screaming at the assistant manager. He may start swearing and arguing with his boss. He may think that he was docked because he was fifteen minutes late on Saturday morning. He may think that good for nothing boss has never treated him fairly. He thinks, I will show him. Not only will I quit, but I will tell everyone not to buy their records here anymore. That will teach him a lesson about not messing around with me! The teen may get his point across, but he will have difficulty getting another job if the boss is unwilling to give him a good reference.

There you have it. That is how five different people may deal with the same situation. They all had different reactions to the same situation. In some cases, the teenagers kept their anger level down. That gave them time to work out the problem. In other cases, the teens let their anger get bottled up inside them. Then, they exploded with very bad results.

It really comes down to the way you think, feel, and behave. Remember, we said earlier that you learned your reactions to situations early in your life, when you were being raised. Although it is hard to change old habits, it can be done. Just as you learned to do things a certain way, you can unlearn them. Then, you can learn a new way of reacting. This new way of reacting will let you deal with people in a better way. Then, you will not have to hurt others, and there will be no bad feelings as a result.

Thinking reasons

Thinking reasons have to do with what you think, what you expect, and what you say to yourself.

1. **Appraisals**

How you see a situation often affects how you feel about that situation. You usually get angry because of the way that you appraise or interpret an event. In other words, you get angry because of the effect things have on you.

Consider this example: You are sitting in the cafeteria. A friend of yours walks by and accidentally spills a Coke on your shirt. She apologizes and seems to feel very badly about it. She says it was an accident, and she is very sorry it happened. You say, "It's okay, clumsy." You playfully pass it off as a mistake.

Suppose the same thing happened, but it was a different student, someone you did not like, someone with whom you recently had an argument. He walks by and spills Coke on you and apologizes. You probably would not take it as well. You would appraise the situation and probably conclude that the guy did it on purpose, even though it could have been a mistake. However, you might not be very forgiving. You probably would take it personally, even though you did not have to look at it that way.

This is one of the more important points you will learn in trying to control your angry feelings. Try not to take things personally, if possible. Attempt to deal with the situation—not the person.

2. **Expectations**

You may be expecting too much of yourself. You may end up taking on too many things at once. You try to do schoolwork, keep a part-time job, play soccer, and more. Then, you find that you do not have enough hours in the day to do it all. You feel disappointed, even frustrated. That can lead to anger. In many ways, it is good to expect a lot of yourself. It is important to set goals. It is a way to get you going toward achieving your goals. However, you should not try to do too much or reach too far. You might be setting yourself up to fail. You probably have enough problems dealing with others in your life and with problems when they arise. You do not have to make more problems for yourself by setting your expectations too high. Unrealistic expectations lead to frustration. Frustration, in turn, results in anger, which robs you of the ability to fulfill your goals.

3. **Self-talk**

We talk to ourselves all the time. One part of our mind is always talking to another part. No, we are not crazy. We all do it, and we do it much of the time we are awake! We even can get into a rage during our talks with ourselves!

What you say to yourself often affects how you feel. Even though what you say to yourself may not always be true, it still affects your attitude. It also affects your reactions to situations and to other people. When you feel something, you talk to yourself about it. You might talk to yourself just before, during, or right after you have that certain feeling.

Think of a situation when something happened that you would normally react to by feeling angry. What you say to yourself then will have a great affect on you. It will affect what you think, how you feel, and how you react.

Now, go back to the example of your friend spilling Coke on you in the cafeteria. You might think to yourself, Lisa—I might like her but is she ever a klutz! Look at her sucking around, whining that it was an accident. She is falling all over herself to apologize. All right, stop it. It was a mistake. Get out of here!

That is an example of self-talk. Those were the things you were saying to yourself while you were going through that situation. Now, here is the other side of the coin. Recall the instance of the student who had a disagreement with you last week who spills Coke on you. You do not like him. He just stumbled slightly as he walked up to you. He spilled a can of Coke on you (just as your friend did in the previous example).

What types of things do you say to yourself? You might say, that —! He did that on purpose. I'll make him pay. He's trying to make me look bad in front of a lot of people. What's worse, he's trying to make it look like an accident. That way, I don't have any grounds to overreact. That does it! I'll settle this right here and now. He started it!

See how important the words are that you say to yourself. They can color your attitude and your thoughts about a situation. In the first case, when your friend spilled Coke on you, you called it a mistake, not a big deal. However, when your enemy spilled the Coke, it was war! The words you say to yourself play a very important role in turning a simple accident into a fistfight. In the end, there will be a lot of grief, possible charges, and a suspension. There even may be serious injury to one or more people (including you).

When you sit and stew about a situation, you replay the memories of bad events in your mind. Such self-talk can keep the anger stewing and build up the hatred inside. This hatred can push you to hurt someone.

The good news is that self-talk can help you to keep a cool head. It also can direct you toward a solution to a problem. It can help you get what you want. It can help you control your anger in many situations. We will talk more about the positive aspects of self-talk later in this book.

Feeling reasons

Feeling reasons are fancy words that mean "how we feel." There are two types of feeling reasons— tension and ill humor.

1. **Tension**

Tension is the feeling of being stressed out. Tension is the feeling of being easily shaken up or bothered by something. There is even a condition known as "tension headache." That is when you worry about so many things that you get a headache. When you work for an extended time or go without sleep for a long time, you become very stressed and irritable. Tension builds up. This might happen over a day or a few days. With tension building up, you become very frustrated and angry. Different parts of your body might feel tense. You might have sore muscles in your chest or your neck, or you might get a headache.

When you are tense, even small problems seem big. Here is an example: You have had a day filled with tension. You are sitting in your bedroom doing your homework when your pencil breaks. That could be enough to make you fire it against the wall. You might say, "To ____ with homework." You even may end up getting a detention for not doing your work. All of this might happen because your pencil broke.

When you are tense, you tend to overreact. So, it is very important that you keep your tension level down. This is especially true if you have a problem with angry feelings.

There are a few ways to keep your tension level down when you are angry. One way is to take a problem-solving approach to a situation. Decide what you want and set goals. Then, stick with those goals. Become task oriented. Try to ignore what the other person is saying or doing. To keep your anger level down, you have to stick to the task. Do not take things personally. Just because someone else has a bad day, that does not mean that he has to ruin your day as well. Sometimes, it is better to stay out of the other teen's way and not get dragged down by his or her foul mood. This way, you also will avoid getting into trouble.

Another way to keep your tension level down is to learn to relax your muscles and your mind. Studies prove that you cannot be tense and relaxed at the same time. By relaxing, you can cope with a hostile or tense situation more easily. We will talk more about relaxation later.

2. **Ill Humor**

How you react to a situation depends on your mood. If you feel down, you have less energy. You may want to just stay in bed and sleep or only watch television and do nothing else. When you are in a bad mood, you tend to be pretty sour toward things that happen to you.

In many cases, when you are in a bad mood, it is because you are taking things too seriously. You are overreacting to situations. Remember, it is important for everyone to have a sense of humor. We need to be able to step back once in a while and see what is really occurring. We need to see the humor in things.

Sometimes, we even can laugh at ourselves. We can laugh at the silly things that we say or do. For example, you were in the gym playing volleyball. You jumped up to block the ball. While you were making this great effort for your team, you fell into the net and knocked over one of the poles. This, of course, would cause a delay in the game. Everyone would laugh at you. Some of them would point their fingers at you, and some might say, "Nice going!" Others might say, "Did you ever look funny. I thought you were going to take off and fly!"

You could react to this situation in different ways. Remember, one of the negative functions of anger is to cover up other feelings. Often, those other feelings should not be covered up. For example, you might get angry when you feel embarrassed. You could easily feel embarrassed in the example here. Before you say, "Go __ yourself," you should do some thinking.

In this example, no one was angry with you for delaying the game. In fact, everyone had a pretty good laugh over it. Some even seemed to be laughing with you instead of at you. What harm do you think would be done if you laughed along with the others? You might say, "Yeah, I really thought I was going to start flying too!"

This situation may never have happened, but similar ones have. In some cases, people ended up fighting. That is too bad because it is not necessary.

Why not see the humor in life once in a while? Even more importantly, why not see the humor in yourself once in a while? Maybe you do stupid or funny things every now and then. Everyone makes mistakes! If you step back and look at some of the things that you have done and the things for which people laughed at you, you would see the humor in them. If you did, you would enjoy yourself more. That does not mean you should not take things seriously anymore. It just means that sometimes it is good to be able to roll with the punches.

Doing (or action) reasons

Doing (or action) reasons are what you actually do when you react to situations that get you upset. The way you react often influences what will happen to you. For example, what would happen if you ignored a situation that you would normally react to by becoming upset? What would happen if you tried to find a peaceful solution that would make everyone happy? You would probably avoid getting into trouble or into a fight even though you might feel like a coward.

What you actually do in a situation will affect your thoughts and feelings about that situation. Your thoughts, feelings, and actions are all tied together. Each one affects the others.

There are two types of actions, avoiding a situation and taking aggressive action.

1. Backing off (avoiding a situation)
Remember the example of your enemy spilling Coke on you? In a backing-off

situation, you might not say anything and pretend it did not happen. You pull back. You also avoid a fight.

You return to class and think about what happened. You might think that you acted like a coward. You think everyone saw what happened. There are ugly dark stains all over your shirt. The drink was cold when it splashed on your shoulder and neck. Some of the other teens even might be aware of the disagreement you two had last week. You look down on yourself for not standing up in that situation. You feel that you did not do the right thing at the right time.

What about that other student? He feels that he has one up on you now. He made you look bad, and you chickened out of a fight. You did not call his bluff. After you think about this for a while, you might consider getting back at him. You might start to plan something hurtful toward him. You might try to confront him and have another fight with him.

Or, you might start spreading rumors about him. In a school environment, rumors can be very damaging. They can be just as bad as punching a guy out. Of course, that depends on the type of rumor you start.

Another choice you have is to dwell on your bad thinking. You might think repeatedly that you are a coward. You even might get depressed over the whole thing. You might develop a low sense of self-worth. You might become very critical about yourself. When this happens, you even might start to feel helpless and hopeless. You might start to question yourself. You might ask yourself why you did not confront the other guy at the time. Maybe, you tell yourself, you really are afraid of him. Maybe he will keep giving you a hard time.

Yet, it is not always best to stay and deal with an issue. In some cases, it is better to walk away and leave well enough alone. After all, sometimes you have to save your own skin. Unfortunately, many of us end up running away. We avoid situations when it is not necessary. We avoid or back off from a situation for the wrong reasons.

2. Hostility (taking aggressive action)

It is difficult to be in a situation where you or the other person might get angry. Return to the example of your enemy who spilled Coke on you. In that situation, if you reacted quickly and became hostile, the conflict would become worse. Anger situations tend to get increasingly worse. A fight usually results from one teen saying something aggressive or threatening to another teen. In this example, your enemy spills Coke on you. Before he can react, you jump up and call him a few choice names.

He responds by saying, "Cool it, man. It was an accident!"
You reply, "Like ___ it was an accident, you ___!"
He comes back with, "Watch who you're calling an ___, ___!"
"Make me, fat boy!" you reply.

The anger from you feeds his anger. It starts to escalate. It becomes more heated. Finally, neither of you can really back out without losing face.

Again, that is not saying that you cannot get into a fight at any time in your life. There are times when your back is to the wall and you have to come out swinging. However, most of the time, you can talk your way out of a sticky situation. You can do it so you do not lose face and the other person does not lose face. You can do it so that everyone ends up feeling pretty good.

Self-talk

We talked earlier about how we think of different situations. We looked at what we expect of ourselves and what we say to ourselves. Although we all talk to ourselves everyday, that does not mean that we are crazy. Because the idea of talking to yourself seems so strange, we will describe it now in more detail. In fact, we will take a long, hard look at your own self-talk.

Before we start, think about what ran through your mind during the last day or so. Much information passed between your ears over the last forty-eight hours. Unfortunately, much of that information was in the form of opinions, beliefs, and judgments. What you really should be concerned with are the facts. Remember that what you think is not always the truth. It is not always the facts as they happened. What you think about is mostly your idea of the facts. Sometimes, it is hard to see the difference between what is true and what is opinion. Your opinions can play tricks with your mind.

Surprising as it may seem, many people never think about what they are thinking. Yet, they go from day to day thinking thoughts. Many of these thoughts affect their opinions and attitudes. Often, what they are thinking about is just not true. These people, just like you, never take the time to think about what they are thinking. They just accept their thoughts. They accept them as fact and believe them to be true. The questions that follow are designed to help you understand how you think. These questions will help you learn what you say to yourself during the course of a day.

So, get ready to go to a quiet place. Take a pen or a pencil to answer the following questions.

ANGER QUESTIONS

PART III: Self-talk

1. When you talk to yourself, how do you encourage yourself? How do you pat yourself on the back? (For example, do you ever tell yourself that you are doing a great job?)

_____

_____

_____

_____

_____

_____

2. Think about what you have been saying to yourself over the last week or two. Do you ever say that you like yourself? Please explain.

_____

_____

_____

_____

_____

_____

3. How would you feel if someone else talked to you the way you talked to yourself? Would you be pleased, insulted, or angry?

_____

_____

4. Talk to the mirror

A. When you are standing in front of a mirror, what do you say to yourself? (For example, the gold medal for brains and great looks goes to me!)

_____

_____

_____

B. How do you look at yourself? (For example, do you criticize yourself for your big stomach, your skinny arms, the acne on your face?)

_____

_____

_____

_____

5. Compliments

A. Have people given you compliments lately? Were they about something that you said or did?

_____

_____

_____

B. In what ways do you compliment yourself? Please list some examples.

_____

_____

_____

_____

6. Embarrassment

A. Has anything like the example mentioned earlier about the teen who fell into the volleyball net ever happened to you? If so, please explain what happened.

_____

_____

_____

_____

_____

_____

B. How did you feel? Were you angry or humiliated? Did you laugh?

_____

_____

_____

_____

_____

C. How do you think you would react if that situation happened today?

_____

_____

_____

_____

7. Putting yourself down

A. What do you say when you get angry or upset with yourself?

_____

_____

_____

_____

B. Are there some common criticisms that you direct toward yourself? What are they?

_____

_____

_____

_____

_____

8. What types of comforting words do you say to yourself after you have been angry with yourself? For example, I guess I messed up big time, but people learn from experience. I won't make that mistake again!

_____

_____

_____

_____

_____

9. Other people

A. What types of things do you say to yourself about other people?

_____

_____

_____

_____

_____

_____

B. Do you make statements such as, "I'm going to rearrange his face. What an ____!"?

_____

_____

_____

_____

_____

_____

10. Do you hear yourself saying things such as, "What a lousy day. No one cares. No one has any use for me, I don't even have any use for myself!"? If you say these kinds of things to yourself, how often do you say them?

_____

_____

_____

_____

_____

_____

_____

Many books have been written about self-talk. Some refer to it as "running tapes in your head." These "tapes" can be good or bad. They are tapes that you play over and over again throughout your life. These self-messages are like repeatedly listening to your mother's voice. She is criticizing you for something that you did when you were younger. On the other hand, the message could be praising you for something you did.

Usually, people who run "good tapes" in their head feel good about themselves. They are calm, and they enjoy life. Some people play tapes about themselves to get down on themselves. They keep themselves feeling angry and feeling like losers. Other people choose to play tapes that offer support. These tapes are forgiving and provide a lot of encouragement. That helps them change and try to do better in the future.

11. Running tapes

A. Do you think you run tapes in your head?

_____

B. If so, are they positive or negative tapes?

_____

_____

C. What are some examples from these tapes?

_____

_____

_____

_____

_____

_____

Anger Log

It is important to keep track of your thoughts and actions if you really want to control your anger. To do that, make photocopies of the Anger Log (page 51) and fill one out every day. Learning about yourself by filling out Anger Logs is a very interesting process. It is also a very important learning situation. The Anger Logs not only will help you find patterns of how you think and feel, they also will show you what tends to make you angry.

You have come to understand how the anger starts in your thoughts, feelings, and actions. You should understand that when anger is starting in you, it is a cue. It means that something is wrong. At that point, you need to try to work your way through the situation with a cool head.

Your Anger Logs will give you clues as to how you really think and feel. They also will let you know how you react to certain situations and how certain events or even words can help you to fly off the handle. They will help you get a grasp on your strengths and weaknesses in the area of anger management. They also will let you know the areas you need to work on to improve your anger control.

As you can see in the Anger Log, there is a place for your name and the date.

There is a line for you to indicate just how angry you were on a scale from one to ten. (One is not so angry and ten is very angry.) Then, there are a few spaces in which you can write down your body signs of anger as you recognize them. For example, "I felt myself getting hot. I felt a pain in my neck, and I felt my hands clench."

There is a space for you to write down your action signs of being angry. For example, "I realized that I was beginning to lose my ability to talk" or "My voice was getting louder. I started pointing my finger."

There are spaces for you to explain the actual provoking situation.

There are spaces for you to explain what you said to yourself (your self-talk) at that time.

There are spaces for you to check off and comment on whether you took a time out (left the situation for a period of time), whether you avoided the situation and kept all the anger inside, if you made the situation worse, or if you focused your anger on someone or something.

There is room to write down your "I" statements, such as, I am feeling stepped on for no reason. I am feeling confused about whether I am right. I am feeling twisted and bent out of shape!

There is a space for you to write down how you handled the situation.

Finally, there is a space to give yourself a rating of one to ten on the amount of self-control you felt afterwards. (One means you are in very good control of yourself; ten indicates a total lack of control.)

Given this explanation and the samples of John Doe's and Michelle Wilde's Anger Logs (see pages 52 and 53), you should have a pretty clear idea of how to record your angry feelings throughout the day. Make photocopies of the Anger Log (page 51) and start filling it out today. The Anger Logs will provide a great deal of information for you.

Anger Log

Name_____ Date_____

Body signs   _____
                1   2   3   4   5   6   7   8   9   10
                (Not so angry)   (Very angry)

Comments:_____

_____

Behavior (Doing or Action) signs:_____

_____

Situation:_____

_____

Self-talk:_____

_____

_____

Did you take a time out?   Yes   No

Comments:_____

_____

Did you avoid the situation and keep all your anger inside?   Yes   No

Comments:_____

_____

Did you make the situation worse?   Yes   No

Comments: _____

_____

Did you focus your anger on someone or something?   Yes   No

Comments: _____

_____

I statement: I am feeling _____

How did you handle the situation? _____

_____

Self-rating of your control afterwards:

                1   2   3   4   5   6   7   8   9   10
                (Not so angry)   (Very angry)

Anger Log

Name ___Michelle Wilde___ Date ___May 3 1995___

Body signs

1	2	3	4	5	6	7	(8)	9	10
(Not so angry)									(Very) angry

Comments: I am pissed!! I hate my mother! What a dumb old cow!! She treats me like a baby!!!

Behavior (Doing or Action) signs: I screamed at her; clenched my jaw, got red in the face/hot, shook, cried/couldn't breathe, later.

Situation: That BITCH won't let me spend the weekend at my boyfriend's cabin. Why?! Why doesn't she trust me!! It's not fair!

Self-talk: She's only being a "mom"; she's doing it because she cares; she doesn't realize that I'm not a kid anymore; she never let my older sister do stuff like this either

Did you take a time out?   (Yes)   No

Comments: Went to my room SLAMMED the door. It felt better to be alone — to think about it/cry by myself.

Did you avoid the situation and keep all your anger inside?   Yes   (No)

Comments: I threw a temper tantrum I guess. It felt good to scream, but maybe it would have been more grown up if I would have been calmer.

Did you make the situation worse?   (Yes)   No

Comments: Screaming turned it into a huge fight. I said things I didn't mean. I should have talked it over calmly.

Did you focus your anger on someone or something?   (Yes)   No

Comments: I told my mother that I hated her. Yet I know she may be right. Maybe I am too young for this weekend trip to

I statement: I am feeling guilty/still angry/upset/confused/sorry.

How did you handle the situation? I didn't handle myself very well. Next time, I'll talk things through like an adult and control my words

Self-rating of your control afterwards:

1	(2)	3	4	5	6	7	8	9	10
(Not so angry)									(Very angry)

Anger Log

Name _John Doe_   Date _2/12/96_

Body signs

1	2	3	4	5	6	7	(8)	9	10
(Not so angry)									(Very angry)

Comments: _chest pounding, breathing fast, stiff neck_

Behavior (Doing or Action) signs: _making fists, shouting, standing very close to the guy_

Situation: _During afterschool basketball game, a guy slammed into me, after I accidentally fouled him._

Self-talk: _He did that on purpose. I should not let him get away with trying to hurt me._

Did you take a time out?   (Yes)   No

Comments: _Only for a few seconds_

Did you avoid the situation and keep all your anger inside?   (Yes)   No

Comments: _I held in as much anger as I could._

Did you make the situation worse?   Yes   (No)

Comments: _I stopped shouting._

Did you focus your anger on someone or something?   (Yes)   No

Comments: _I blamed him because I could have been hurt._

I statement: I am feeling _challenged. He probably wants to fight me._

How did you handle the situation? _I stopped shouting and told him, "So now we're even."_

Self-rating of your control afterwards:

1	2	(3)	4	5	6	7	8	9	10
(Not so angry)									(Very angry)

53

Once you have filled out the Anger Logs for a number of days, you will have a great deal of information. That information will give you some idea about how you think and feel in certain situations and how that may contribute to your decision to feel angry. The next step will be to see how you can change your views or your actions in those situations. Remember, in some cases it is okay to be angry! However, you must realize that there is a different way to act. Even though it was okay to feel angry in a situation, that does not mean that what you did or said was right. When you react differently, you will find that you will get different results. In fact, it is best to try to work out a halfway point. If you can work out your problems, then everyone wins without anyone losing face.

Your Anger Logs will help you begin to understand your own feelings, thoughts, and actions. You will be looking at them to find patterns in why you act, think, and feel the way that you do. That will give you some explanation for your actions. Then, you will begin to see that you could have done things differently to get different results. You could get these different results by using other words, by using a little more calmness, or by using a little more or less body language.

People seem to pay more attention to the "nonverbal" (or body language) than they do to the actual words. The following is a simple and quick list to consider when you are dealing with another person concerning an important issue. We found it on a yellowed sheet of paper while we were compiling this book. We do not know who the author is but thought it too valuable not to share with you. Keep this list in mind when you are watching other people interacting. Not only does it contain some cues on body language, it also contains important "voice cues."

Voice cues

1) Loudness: Too loud? Too soft?
2) Clearness of speech: Can you understand each of the words?
3) Speech flow: Smooth? Too fast? Too jerky?
4) Time person speaks: Too short? Too long-winded?

Body cues

1) Eye Contact: Not looking at the other person enough? Staring at the other person too long
2) Posture: Stiff? Uptight? Too relaxed? Belligerent? Submissive? Sloppy?
3) Gestures: Too many? Too few? Postures do not match the words that are being spoken?

4) Facial expressions: Deadpan? Overdone? Eyes narrowed? Lips tight? Face flushed?

5) Body Movement: Stiff? Jerky? Body parts (such as hands, arms, or head) shaking?

A teenager may say, "I went down to talk to Angela to try to work things out smoothly, without a fight. I got into a fight anyway because she pushed me to the limit."

In many cases, a teen may not realize that she pushed Angela into a corner with her words, her tone of voice, or her actions (or body language). She gave the other teen very little choice but to lash out through her own words or actions. That is just it! We often do not realize how we come across to other people. We think we know, but we cannot read minds. At best, we are only second-guessing the other person.

You have learned how important it is to look through the other person's eyes. By taking the other person's point of view, you can see what makes him or her react the way he or she does. Maybe what the other person is saying is right! Maybe what you are saying or doing is making the situation worse. Your actions might be increasing his or her fears and anger. You have to pay attention to your own body language when you are in a situation that may get tense. You must be aware of what you say, how you say it, what you do, and how you do it!

It is best to stay calm, cool, and collected in tense situations. The old saying, "Cooler heads prevail" is true. In fact, remaining calm, and even "modeling calmness" to the other person is a great way to "save face." Trying to focus on what the problem is could save you many verbal insults, fights, hurt feelings, and possible injuries.

4 How to Manage Your Anger

So far, we have been talking about what anger is, what causes anger, and the good and bad uses of anger. You have been brave in answering a lot of questions about yourself and your anger. You have taken a hard look at your past to see how anger made a difference in your early life. You have looked at how you think and feel and what you do when you get angry. You also have examined your self-talk about your angry feelings. Those are big steps. Believe it or not, you are well on your way to improving your control over your anger. After all, the first step in doing something the right way is to learn how to do it. Until now, you have learned many "school-like" lessons about anger. Besides, the questions you have answered have related anger to you! They have put the focus on your angry feelings. You have become aware that your angry feelings are a problem for you.

Now, we will look at some ways that you can manage your anger. This does not mean that you should get rid of all your anger. As we mentioned, anger does have some good uses. However, we will look at some ways that you can take control of your anger. Once you know how to do that, you can be angry when you should be, but you also can avoid angry outbursts by controlling your bottled-up angry feelings.

To better understand what bottled-up angry feelings are, picture an anger bag. Imagine a bag with a spout on it. Angry feelings and thoughts are poured into the top of the bag, and the bag fills up quickly. There is a leaky faucet at the bottom that drips out sarcasm and insults. Needless to say, it is never healthy to have a full bag of anger. The bag should be emptied regularly to keep angry feelings from building up. Remember, if you operate at low-to-medium levels of anger, you can better cope with any situation. It is best to avoid high levels of anger.

Another way to understand bottled-up angry feelings is to picture a stick of dynamite with a short fuse on it. That stick of dynamite is you. There is a match at the end of the fuse. That match is an angry situation. This is a problem that needs to be resolved. You know how hard it is to find a solution to a problem if you do not have time to think about it or work it out. Once that fuse is lit, you only have a few seconds. That can be very frustrating. We have already talked about how frustration often leads to verbal or physical aggression. What if you were given a problem and had enough time to work out an answer? What if the fuse were lit, but it was a very long fuse? Then, it would take some time to reach the dynamite. You would have enough time to work out a solution to the problem. You could put out the fuse before it reached the dynamite and exploded.

"Impulsive" people often react before thinking about the consequences. You might say an impulsive person reacts before even trying to solve the problem. These people have short fuses.

To control your anger, you have to make your fuse longer. You have to give yourself more time to solve a problem. Controlling your anger means working out an answer to a problem without becoming frustrated. The idea is to keep your problem-solving abilities high and your frustration low. That is what we mean when we talk about keeping the anger bag only partly filled at any time.

When you think about it, people with short fuses lead pretty miserable lives. Could one of them be you? If so, maybe your relationships are not very happy ones. Maybe people do not like to be around you. Maybe you frequently get into trouble with your parents or teachers. Maybe your short temper makes your relationship with others that much worse because you insult them and are often in a bad mood. You may think that other people are always getting on your nerves. However, did you ever think that maybe other people might find you getting on their nerves? That would make life a big battle. It would be very draining. It would make for a lonely, unhappy existence.

There is a way to avoid that kind of miserable existence. You can enjoy life more by making your fuse longer!

When we talked about what causes anger, we mentioned three things:

1. Outside reasons (things that happen to you)
2. Inside reasons (what you think of a situation, what you expect, what you say to yourself, tensions and ill humor)
3. Doing (or action) reasons (the things that you do as a result of the outside and inside reasons)

Dealing with outside reasons

There is little or nothing you can do about outside reasons. Those situations will keep on happening every day. Nothing is going to change that. They always will be there.

However, there are some things that you can do to make those outside reasons less difficult. For example, you can stop hanging around the loudmouths and troublemakers. You know who they are. They are in every school. Just being associated with them can get you in trouble. They can influence your attitudes and opinions. They can give you a bad outlook on life. If you hang around with them, teachers, parents, and friends may look at you in a bad light because they may judge you guilty by association.

Additionally, there are situations that you know will get you in trouble. What if you teasingly told the school bully that you dated his girlfriend last night. What do you think would happen? He might start a fight. You might end up punching him or getting punched. Now, you no doubt know enough not to tease the school bully, but this example shows that there are situations that you realize you should avoid. There are situations that you recognize as accidents waiting to happen.

As you can see from these examples, you can make some external situations less risky. You can control some of the situations that you normally might react to by becoming angry. You also can control the situations where someone may become angry at you! That is a start. That is a big step toward managing your anger. That is one way you are starting to have control of yourself so that you can enjoy life more. It is the beginning of a sense of control for you. You can choose to start being in the right places at the right times. That is quite a change from being in the wrong places at the wrong times.

A second way you can try to cut down on getting mixed up in angry situations is not to start fights and not to give others a reason to hate you. An example of this would be calling a group of bodybuilders or jocks "goofs." Maybe you give a teacher a hard time so that you can get a laugh from the rest of your classmates. In these situations, those people could end up giving you a hard time! They could come back and say or do nasty things to you. You could react to this by becoming angry. That could lead to a confrontation. There could be a fight in which everyone would lose.

Stop for a few minutes and look at how this information applies to you. Think back over the many angry situations in your past. Think of one or two times when you got into a really heated argument or a physical confrontation.

You might not have realized that you were causing the situation to occur. Looking back though, perhaps you were making it happen. Take the time now to:

1. Describe an anger situation.

_____

_____

_____

_____

_____

2. Answer the question: What did I do in that situation that might have brought on the argument?

_____

_____

_____

_____

Now, look at all of your Anger Logs. Look at the self-talk. You probably can see a pattern in what you say to yourself when you get into angry situations. You probably can tell when you are becoming angry. You are acquiring a sense of how you feel and what happens to your body when you get angry. Write in the spaces below some of the self-talk that tends to make you angry. In other words, write those things that you say to yourself which may act to escalate your anger, like bringing a pot of water from a slow simmer to a boil.

_____

_____

_____

_____

_____

_____

Remember, there are good points about anger as well as bad points. Anger can give you energy. It can give you a sense of being in control. It can help you recognize unfairness and communicate your feelings. Unfortunately, anger also can keep you from thinking with a clear head. If you become overdependent on anger as a reaction, you may tend to feel anger instead of embarrassment or humiliation in certain situations. Anger may lead to aggression.

The ABCs of how emotions develop

When a situation occurs, you may have a wonderful experience with good feelings, a bad experience with angry feelings, or something in the middle. Basically:

"A" stands for the "Activating" event or "trigger" in a situation.
"B" stands for the "Belief" or self-talk about that situation.
"C" stands for the "Consequences" or the "end result—your reactions in that situation.

We have already discussed self-talk and how our thoughts influence our understanding of what is occurring. It is important enough to discuss it again. An example of this is the situation where someone spills Coke on you. If that person were a friend of yours, then the breakdown probably would be as follows: The activating event (A) is the teenager spilling Coke on you. The belief or self-talk (B) is that he or she is a friend and therefore would not do it on purpose. The consequence (C) is that you do not get angry (or, in some cases, you remain calm, laugh it off as a joke, and make a comment such as, "Good move, genius! Look what you've done!").

If, however, the "Coke spiller" were someone you did not like, then the activating event would be the same. Your belief or self-talk about the situation would be that he did it on purpose. Your belief or self-talk would add to your starting to feel hot (or angry). The consequence (or end result) may be for you to respond in an aggressive manner.

Look back at some of your Anger Logs and try to do an A-B-C to explain some of those situations and your reactions to them.

The degree of readiness your body has to react to various feelings at any given time varies. You may have a very low level of focused attention or readiness to almost any situation. For example, when you first wake up in the morning, your head is groggy. You cannot think straight, and you move slowly. In the middle of a basketball game, however, you are very highly focused. You are alert, and your adrenalin is pumping. You are ready for anything. When your state of readiness is high, your heart rate increases, your blood pressure increases, you sweat more, there is more muscle tension, and you take quick breaths.

When you are in the middle of a basketball game or if you are extremely afraid or very angry, you become highly focused. When you are highly focused (or overly prepared), your effectiveness may decrease. For example, you may focus on a pass and become more keen on making a basket. Likewise, if you become highly focused when you are angry, you may narrow your attention down to attacking the other person. During the heat of the battle, during that basketball game, your mind really does not pay attention to what someone in the stands may be saying. You are focused on getting that basketball into the hoop. Likewise, when you are highly focused or pay too much attention to angry feelings, your mind focuses on verbally hurting or physically attacking someone (being on the offensive). As a result, you cannot think clearly. You cannot think of other options. It disrupts your regular thinking.

What you may not realize is that if you are angry and focused on the anger (and perhaps on attacking the other person) you may not be very effective. Take boxers for example. They bob around the ring and tease each other into making mistakes. The teasing

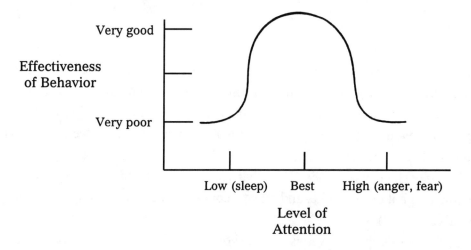

makes one of the boxers angry. He lashes out blindly, leaving himself wide open for a left hook.

There is a middle ground, a best level of attention or readiness. This exists for sports, social activities, problem solving, and even anger situations. Look at the graph above.

The left side of the graph shows your effectiveness in terms of doing, thinking, feeling, and perceiving range from very good to very poor. Along the bottom of the graph, you can see that your level of attention or readiness can be low (when you are sleeping or just waking), best (in the middle ground), or high (when you are feeling extreme anger or fear). On the graph, there is a horseshoe-like line. That line indicates that when your level of attention or readiness is very low, your effectiveness is very low, as well. However, if you are overly attentive, you are not at your best level of effectiveness, either. You should try to be right in the middle of an angry situation, with a medium level of readiness or attention.

Not everyone's level of readiness or attention is the same. A situation that might throw you into a high level of readiness might put someone else at a medium level. The best way to get to know the type of situations that you react to by becoming highly focused or overly prepared and what situations that only provoke a low level of readiness is to pay attention to your reactions over a period of time. You have been doing this all along with your Anger Logs. Check at the top of an Anger Log where you indicated how much self-control you thought you had. That rating is similar to the level of attention, focus, and state of readiness that we are talking about here.

Lowering your readiness level

An important point to remember is that if you feel you are at a high level of attention, too focused, or feel very angry, then do not even attempt to continue with the situation. If at all possible, try to take a "time out." Time out simply means that you leave the situation, if you can, for a short period of time. That allows you to calm down and bring your anger level down to a medium or best level.

Sometimes it is not possible to take a time out, especially if you are in class. However, there are many times that you can. If you found out that another student was going through your personal stuff in your locker, you would become angry. It might be best to calm yourself down a bit before confronting this person.

Here is another example of a time out. You have a grudge with another guy and he tries to provoke you around teachers and other students. You might feel that if you do not stand up to him, you will look bad. You might lose face because you did not accept his challenge right then and there. Instead, you could tell him that you want to discuss it with him later.

A time out can be used to look at the facts. Say, for example, someone in your class comes to you and accuses you of being a thief. You may want to take a time out and find out why he is calling you a thief. For example, if you discovered that an enemy of yours was feeding your accuser false information, then you would know enough not to confront him or be angry with him. You could probably go to him with a cool head and explain that he was told false information. Then, you could go to your enemy and confront him with his lies. This approach is far better than overreacting and fighting the person who called you a thief.

Keep in mind that anger management does not mean just managing your anger. It also means thinking about the other person's point of view. You know that the guy who confronted you in front of others must be pretty pumped up, that he has to be very highly prepared to do battle. You know that he is very angry and probably cannot think straight. If you know that much, you also know that you have some choices.

1. You could be forced or tricked into fighting with him right then and there, which means you may get charged, suspended, or beaten up.

2. You could be a coward and run away, lose face, be embarrassed, and get a new reputation.
3. Since you know the other guy is very angry (overly focused) and probably cannot think clearly, you should allow him to take a time out before the two of you get together to resolve your problems.

Chances are you can solve the problem without either of you getting hurt, if you can talk when you both have clear heads. A time out is a good way to lower everyone's level of readiness to the point that you can start to communicate with cool heads and start the process of problem solving.

Relaxation

Another way to lower your anger level is to relax. However, you have to learn how to relax. With practice, you will be able to relax right in the middle of an anger-provoking situation. You can learn to take a short time out and use that time to relax. Doing that will give you a cool head and the ability to handle almost any situation.

Here are some ways to relax.

1. **Take deep breaths.** One type of relaxation is to stand where you are and take three or four deep breaths. Breathe in; hold it for five or six seconds; then, breathe out. Wait a few seconds and take another deep breath. Amazingly, many people find that doing this tends to lower their anxiety, as well as their anger levels.

2. **Pause.** This simply means to wait a minute or so before answering a question. In some cases, people count from one to ten to themselves. This is a way to make the fuse longer. It gives you more time to react and helps you stick to the task. It helps you develop self-control.

3. **Calm yourself with self-talk.** Say things to yourself such as, stick with the problem. Don't take it personally. This is not going as badly as I thought. Or, I see what the problem is. It should be easy to work out.

4. **Listen to relaxation tapes.** Relaxation tapes are an important part of relaxation training. Make an effort to buy or borrow a copy of a relaxation tape. You may want to ask your guidance counselor if there is a tape that you may borrow. If you cannot get a copy, at least find a tape of soft, soothing music. Listen to the tape at least once a day early in the morning or in the evening just before you go to sleep.

5. **Learn the muscle tense-and-release cycle.** This way of relaxing consists of tensing an area of your body, your arm for example, and then relaxing it. Try it on your lower arm. Make a fist, clench it very hard and hold it for five seconds. Then, relax and let your hand open up and rest for a few seconds. Once again, clench your hand and form a fist and tighten it for another five seconds. Then, release the tension and allow your hand to open up again. Do this tense-and-release cycle on each of the major muscles in your body. When you are finished, you should feel very relaxed and warm.

6. **Use imagery relaxation.** This involves sitting and clearing your mind of outside thoughts and concentrating on your body, focusing on feelings of warmth and heaviness, and breathing.

Learning to relax is wonderful. Once you have learned the skills of relaxation, you will find them useful for the rest of your life. Before you learn any relaxation, however, there are a few general rules to follow.

1. You must be in a quiet area—a place that is free from loud noises.

2. Calm yourself down. This may mean taking a few deep breaths to start to relax. It may mean trying to calm your mind by pushing out thoughts about your schoolwork, your friends, or about what is upsetting you. Try to push all of that out of your mind and focus on the quiet around you.

3. Try to get as comfortable as you can. If you have a tight belt on, loosen it. Take off your watch or any rings that fit tightly. Sit comfortably in a chair or put your head down on a table. Do not cross your legs; it cuts off the blood and makes it difficult to relax. If you are in your bedroom, lay down on your bed on your back, face the ceiling.

4. Put on a relaxation tape or soft music and decide that for the next twenty minutes or so that you are going to sit or lie there and not think about anything else. The only concern you will have is listening to the tape. You can get back to the noise of the real world and all of your challenges and headaches later. For now, this time is just for you.

5. Close your eyes.

6. When you have finished relaxing, do not spring up off the chair or bed. Your body has been relaxed and needs to move around slowly at first. Be gentle with yourself. Slowly open and close your hands. Slowly, move your arms and legs. In general, move about slowly for the first few minutes after you have relaxed.

You will find that relaxation can help you with your anger management. Remember, people tend to become tense in anger situations. Much of that comes from tight muscles. We store up tension in different parts of our body. Tension only makes things worse when we are in anger situations. Tension shortens the fuse on our stick of dynamite.

By learning relaxation, your muscles will become more smooth than tense. Having smooth muscle tone during a situation has many advantages. It helps you lengthen your fuse. It helps you take a problem-solving approach to the situation, and it helps you avoid taking things personally. It gives you a clear head and helps you remain calm so you can assess the situation.

Combining relaxation with a short time out can give you a cool head and the ability to handle almost any situation.

Relaxation log

Just like the Anger Log, there is a Relaxation Log. It is easier to complete than the Anger Log. On a scale of one to ten, indicate how your body felt before relaxing and how your body felt after relaxing. Also, on a scale of one to ten, rate how your mind was before and after you relaxed.

Remember, earlier we talked about "Inside Reasons" of why you may feel angry. Depending on how your day is going, the mood you are in, or your attitudes about another person, you will react differently—maybe in an angry manner. In a given situation, your mind may be quite relaxed and calm or your mind may be racing and you feel angry.

Make photocopies of the Relaxation Log (page 67). Then, begin filling out a Relaxation Log everyday. Listen to your relaxation tapes in the morning or at night before you go to sleep. Record your information in the Relaxation Log following each time you listen to the tape.

Do not forget to fill out a Relaxation Log every day.

Relaxation Log

Name_____ Date_____

Before relaxing

Time: _____

Body: |_____
         1   2   3   4   5   6   7   8   9   10
         (Very relaxed)   (Very tense)

Mind: |_____
         1   2   3   4   5   6   7   8   9   10
         (Very calm)   (Racing/angry)

After relaxing

Time: _____

Body: |_____
         1   2   3   4   5   6   7   8   9   10
         (Very relaxed)   (Very tense)

Mind: |_____
         1   2   3   4   5   6   7   8   9   10
         (Very calm)   (Racing/angry)

Comments:_____

_____

_____

_____

Thinking controls

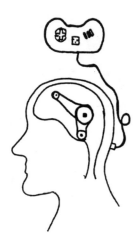

Inside reasons are related to the way you think. They include appraisal, expectation, and self-talk. They are also related to your emotional state, such as your body feeling tense or your mind being in ill humor.

Your thoughts and feelings and actions usually are all tied together. If you look carefully at situations that tend to make you angry, if you start to recognize the physical signs that your body gives you, and if you understand how powerful your self-talk can be, you can learn how to handle angry situations. Your Anger Logs contain this information. Take another look at entries in your Anger Log and try to find some patterns in your behavior. Then, think about how you can change that behavior.

There are some common thinking mistakes that people often make. If you know what thinking mistakes are, you will have a better chance of avoiding them. Here is a list of the twelve biggest thinking mistakes:

1. All or nothing thinking

This means you tend to see things as either black or white. Either something is all right or it is all wrong. If a friend is five minutes late for an appointment, you assume she will not show up at all. If your boyfriend (or girlfriend) said that they would see you on Thursday and you do not see them on Thursday, then you think that it means he (or she) does not want to see you ever.

2. Overgeneralization

This happens when you view one bad situation as a never-ending pattern of bad situations. An example would be if someone picked on you on the way to class. You then want to avoid going to class because you think that you always will be in this situation.

3. Mental filter

This happens when you pick out one bad thing and dwell on it to the point that everything seems bad. The only things that filter in are bad things.

4. Not counting on the good things

When something good happens to you, you say it was just luck. When something bad happens to you, however, you consider it the usual. For some reason, good things do not count. For example, you might say, "Yeah, I scored three points in the game today, but I have not scored any points in the last three games!"

5. Jumping to conclusions

This happens when you decide that something is bad even though you do not know for sure.

6. Mind reading

You think that someone is either being mean to you or does not like you, and you do not even bother to check it out. For example, you are walking across the school yard and you notice that the principal is looking at you. Because he is staring, you think he does not like you. The fact might be that he is staring into space and thinking about something else and not paying any attention to you.

7. The fortune-teller mistake

This happens when you believe that something will turn out badly and you treat it as fact. An example is believing that you are not going to get that part-time job. If you go to the interview in a bad mood, you might think that you already have lost the chance before you even go into the room. This usually ends up coming true because you go into the meeting feeling lousy. You think the interviewer has already judged you. You do not make a good impression, and the interviewer says you did not get the job. What you have done is "set yourself up." You might have had a decent chance, but because of your attitude and the way you presented yourself, the boss is not willing to take a chance on you.

8. Magnifying or minimizing

This is often called the binocular trick. Previously, we talked about downplaying the positive. That is, when something good happens, you think it does not count. For example, four different people tell you that you played a great basketball game the other night. You do not pay much attention to those positive comments because you are thinking about making plans for the weekend. In other words, when something positive happens to you, you tend to minimize it, like looking through binoculars backwards. When you do that, everything looks smaller or minimized. Bad events, however, become magnified, like looking through the binoculars the right way. You make a poor mark on a test at school. It does not matter that you are doing great on all the other tests and that most of the other students also made bad marks on this test. A small problem seems a lot bigger, and you spend more time dwelling on it.

9. **Reasoning how you feel**

An example would be, "Because I feel bad, bad things must happen to me. There must be a reason for me to feel bad. If not, I might as well make one up!" This could lead you to dwell on the bad things.

10. **Should statements**

You may say, "I should" or "I shouldn't." The same could be said for the "musts" and the "oughts" in your talk. You often say things such as, "I should have taken that course," or, "I should have done my job better," or, "I must exercise today!" What often happens is that you feel guilty. Because you felt there was a need to have done it in the past or to do it in the future, you end up feeling guilty because whatever it was, you did not do it. There was probably a good reason why you did not do it. However, that does not matter. All you feel is the hurt and guilt. More importantly is directing these "shoulds," "musts," and "oughts" toward others. When this happens, you usually feel frustrated. You end up feeling resentment and anger toward them. The self-talk might be, "He should have asked me to go to the game with him. He never thinks about me, and I always do things for him. It must be because he does not like me. He is no hotshot. I do not like him much either."

11. **Labeling and mislabeling**

An example of this may be when you see a coach yelling at one of his players, and you think (label him), what a fool! What is his problem? In reality, he may be a great coach and a very caring person. However, you now have labeled him in your mind as being a "mean fool." In fact, because he really is a nice person, you have mislabeled him. You did not accurately assess him. The problem with labels is that they usually "stick" to the person. If you gave somebody a "bad label" in your mind, then, it becomes very difficult to change the way you feel or what you think about them.

12. **Taking it personally**

This happens when you take the blame for some bad event even though it was not your fault. An example would be the following tape you play in your head. It's my fault she's sick. I shouldn't have asked her to come over! Or, it's my fault that we lost the game. I'm a jinx. I bring trouble wherever I go! Another tape may be, it's my fault; I gave the teacher a hard time yesterday, and today the whole class has to stay in.

Signposting anger (Becoming aware that you are getting angry)

Signposting is a thought-stopping procedure. (It is useful especially when you are in an anger situation and you start to become angry.) Recall the discussion about how you can use your body reactions to indicate to your mind that you are becoming angry. We talked about things such as feeling tension in your neck, feeling your fists clench, raising the tone of your voice, and talking louder.

In thought-stopping, when you recognize these body cues, and you recognize the feelings you get that indicate you are becoming angry, that is the time to say "stop" to yourself. It is like seeing a stop sign on the street. It is a signal for you to realize that you are becoming very angry, that you should slow down and consider what is happening and what you are saying to yourself. Give yourself a chance to relax before deciding how to respond to the situation.

Think back to the situation where someone spilled Coke on you. Think about your self-talk in that situation. Perhaps you said to yourself, he did it on purpose, that idiot. He is trying to make me look bad! I will fix him!

Better self-talk would be, that fool, he spilled Coke on me. He should be more careful in the future or else I will not be willing to pass it off as an accident. Or, ____, that is the guy who does not like me. I wonder if he did that on purpose?

In the first example, you already have had the trial, delivered the verdict, and are about to hang the guy (by attacking him). In the next examples, however, you are still in the process of having the trial. You are unsure whether it was an accident. Thinking that way will give you time to gather more facts or question him before reacting. After all it might have been an accident. There is no sense in overreacting.

Think about some situations that you have been in where you might have avoided a conflict by using better self-talk.

Staging (Dealing with an anger situation by taking it one step at a time)

Earlier, you saw how thinking mistakes can affect your self-talk in anger situations. Although your self-talk can stir things up, it also can be used to keep your angry feelings under control.

"Staging," or breaking an event into smaller parts, can help you think and act at a medium or best level, to keep the fuse on that stick of dynamite long.

Basically, when you are in an anger situation, you can stage the event by breaking it into four parts:

- Preparing for the situation
- Impact and confronting
- Coping with feelings
- Reflecting on the situation afterwards

1. Preparing for the situation

When you know that you are going to be facing a situation that will make you angry, you can use appropriate self-talk to help you keep your cool. Here are some examples of self-talk that can help you keep down your anger level.

— What is it that I have to do?

— I know I can work out a plan to handle this.

— Remember, stick to the facts and do not take it personally.

— I can manage the situation.

— There will not be any need for fists flying. I can work this out.

— Try not to take this too seriously.

— Easy does it.

— Time to take a few deep breaths.

— Feel comfortable, relaxed, and together.

2. Impact and confronting

These two phases of anger can happen gradually or quite suddenly. You know how to recognize your anger through body cues and the types of things you say to yourself. When

help you through the impact and confronting stage.

— Stay calm now.

— Just continue to relax.

— As long as I keep my cool, everything is okay, and I am in control.

— Roll with the flow. Do not get bent out of shape.

— I do not have to prove myself

— There is no point in getting mad. There is going to be an easy answer.

— Do not make any more out of this than I have to.

— I am not going to let her get to me.

— Now, hold on. Do not jump to conclusions, and do not expect the worst.

— That other person is angry, and if I start to get angry, I will just be banging my head against the wall. I will have to figure this one out for both of us!

— What he says does not matter. I am on top of the situation. It is under control, and I can keep it that way.

3. Coping with feelings

When you are in an ugly situation and there is no end in sight, you get tense. Here are some things that you can say to yourself to help you cope with this difficult phase of the confrontation.

— My knuckles are starting to feel tight. It is time to relax and slow things down.

— It is just not worth it to get angry.

— Yeah, maybe I have a right to be angry, but I will keep the lid on it for now.

— Let me take a look at this issue—point by point. Maybe that will help resolve this mess.

— I am not going to get pushed around. However, I am not going to lose my head either.

— Treat each other with respect. Maybe that is the way to get this thing solved.

— Okay, maybe we are both right. Let me see what he is saying.

— He is probably going to get very angry and mess up. I am not going to do that.

— Take it easy. Do not get pushy.

4. **Reflecting on the situation afterwards**

The situation is over, and you are either patting yourself on the back for how you dealt with it, or you are still furious and plotting a way to get revenge on the other person. Here are some examples of things to say to yourself when the situation is not over yet.

— Oh, forget it. Thinking about it only makes me upset. It will get me nowhere.

— This is a difficult situation. It will take time to straighten it out, but it will straighten out.

— I will try to shake it off. I will not let it interfere with the rest of my life.

— Can I laugh about it? Can I find something funny about it? If I can, then it is not that serious.

When the situation is over, it is time for some self-praise. Here are some examples of self-praise.

— I handled that one pretty well. It worked. I am a hero!

— That was not as hard as I thought.

— Hey, that went over pretty well. I could have been a lot more upset, but it was not worth it.

— I got through that one without getting very angry.

— I guess I have been getting upset over this for too long even when it was not necessary. I am getting better at this all the time.

These examples should give you some direction. It is important, however, for you to develop your own self-talk, to develop your own sentences to say to yourself at each of the staging phases. Some statements work better than others. Find some that work for you.

A useful part of this staging process is that it tells you at what point in the situation you are weak and start to fall apart. It shows you the areas where you need more work.

What would you do?

Here is a common situation, which may happen to you. Following the situation are different examples of self-talk (depending on how you interpret or understand that situation).

Someone borrows your favorite board game. When he returns it, there are a few pieces missing. Here are some interpretations of that situation:

1. He may have taken the pieces from the game on purpose.
2. The pieces accidentally got left out when they were put back into the box.
3. You made a mistake counting them.

Given that situation, either someone did something mean to you on purpose, which means you have a right to be angry, or you might have made a mistake. It might be wise to recount the game pieces before you jump to conclusions. On the other hand, the person who had your game could have made an honest mistake and did not mean to rip you off.

Depending on how you understand the situation, depending on your self-talk, your reactions may include:

- confronting the guy to whom you loaned the game and getting into a raging argument with him
- counting the game pieces before deciding on a course of action
- telling the other guy that some pieces are missing
- asking the other teen for a reason why there are pieces missing

Everything is not always as it seems. In a given situation, you should wait and not just accept the first self-talk that comes into your mind. Wait for a few moments and consider other possible meanings of that situation before reacting. Maybe, it was an honest mistake. Maybe, it was done in fun and not meant to hurt you.

Communicating feelings

It is important in any situation to tell the other person up front that there is no need for threats. Just tell her that you are feeling very upset and want to work the situation out peacefully. That should be enough to let her know that you are willing to try to find a peaceful solution to the problem. She may not realize how much she is upsetting you. In many cases, simply telling the other person how you feel may be enough to make her back down. Avoid threats! They only will make you and the other person more angry.

This is just as important and, some people believe, even more important for males. As males grow up, they may not get the opportunity to express a variety of feelings. Many guys may get lectures from their parents or friends such as, "Don't cry. Don't show you are hurt. Only wimps show they are afraid. Don't get mad, get even (be aggressive)," and other messages. The problem is, we all feel hurt, are afraid, or become upset from time to time. This is natural. It is also natural to express these feelings when we communicate. It may take some practice for guys because many are not used to allowing themselves to do it.

Calming others

By now, you are probably well on your way to controlling your temper in many situations. At the very least, you should notice improvements in your ability to stick to a task, not to take things personally, and to work your way through sticky situations. By using relaxation and self-talk, you have probably reached a point where you can remain fairly calm throughout most bad situations.

Now it is time to learn how to make the other person (the person who is feeling angry toward you) feel calm and reduce his or her angry feelings. There are six rules to follow in your attempts to calm others in angry situations: model calmness, encourage talking, listen openly, show understanding, reassure the other person, and help save face.

1. **Model calmness**

Give an outward appearance of being calm. Use a calm voice. Use nonthreatening gestures. Talk softly in low tones. The reason for acting this way is because it is hard to stay angry with someone who does not get angry back. If you react to an angry situation in a calm manner, the chances are the other person who is yelling at you and who is caught up in the heat of battle also will tend to relax. Keep in mind that the opposite holds true: if you become excited and aggressive, that only will make the other person more and aggressive, as well.

2. Encourage talking

Do not let the other person stare at you in silence. Ask questions. Get him or her to talk out the frustrations. Start communicating! Try to get the other teenager to talk to you instead of yelling or screaming at you. Get him to explain to you why he is angry, and then, try to get him to work with you to solve the problem.

3. Listen openly

Show the other person that you are listening to what she is saying. Keep eye contact with her and nod your head to let her know that you understand what she is saying. Try to avoid interrupting her while she is talking. Listen carefully to what she says. Try to read between the lines to tell if there is some other theme or agenda that concerns her that she is not telling you, or that she may not even realize herself.

4. Show understanding

This can be done very easily by telling the other person that you understand what he is saying. Say things such as, "I see what you mean."

Another way to show that you understand what he is saying is by paraphrasing. This simply means that you tell him what he has told you in different words. Say something such as, "Now, let me see if I've got this straight. You are angry with me because. . ." All you have to do is restate what he told you.

You can also show someone that you understand what is going on by focusing on his or her feelings. This is called "empathy." Empathy means focusing more on what the other person is feeling than on what the person is saying. A good way to show empathy for the other person is to try to put yourself in his shoes. Ask yourself, if I were that person and that happened to me, how would I feel?

To understand how the other person feels, do not just pay attention to her words. Note her body language. Pay attention to her breathing rate, her gestures, her posture, and her face. These can give you clues about how angry and emotional she may be at that particular time.

If you can put yourself in her shoes and feel what she is going through, then, tell her! By having empathy for the other person and telling her that, you are going a long way toward getting rid of all the angry feelings between the two of you. From that point, it is fairly simple to solve the problem.

5. **Reassure the other person**

This means telling the other person that answers do exist, that not every option has been examined yet. The situation does not have to result in a fight. You might say things such as:

— It is okay. We can work this out.

— I agree with you. It is a problem. What can we do to solve it?

—Okay, I am willing to work with you to solve this mess and straighten it out.

By using these statements or similar ones, you appear less threatening to the other person, and you offer hope that a solution can be reached. These phrases should be offered sincerely. It is obvious that your body language and your talking must match. For example, it would not do any good to say you are willing to work on it if you are waving your fist in his face.

6. **Helping save face**

It does not do anyone any good for you to back the other person into a corner. If you back an animal into a corner, it will come out fighting, biting, or swinging. Another human being will react in the same way. It is best to give him a way to save face and back off gradually. Try to avoid audiences. Try to avoid embarrassing the other person. It will take a lot of self-control for you to remain calm through this process. However, if you do not remain calm, everything you have learned until now is lost.

Try to make the other person see that he or she is not angry with you personally, but that he or she is angry with something you did. Your actions have caused him to get angry, not you.

Would it be so hard to say that you did something wrong? No one is perfect. Everyone makes mistakes and everyone does wrong things once in a while. So what? Swallow your pride if, in fact, you did do something wrong. It does not make you any less of a person. It certainly does not mean that you have to go around apologizing for everything that you do. However, if you really do something wrong, own up to it and try to make amends. There are people who have ended up being fast friends after their first argument.

Look how far you have come

In the spaces below, write down any improvements you see in yourself or feel or think about yourself. You have taken many big steps toward self-control. You should be starting to think about, feel, and even see a difference. You should be able to see the difference in your dealings with others and how they deal with you.

_____

_____

_____

_____

_____

_____

_____

_____

Start to look on the positive side of your life. To help you do this, list five good things that happened to you today. Then, do this on a daily basis on a separate sheet of paper that you keep with this book.

1._____

2._____

3._____

4._____

5._____

Recognizing your anger

Based on your Anger Logs and what you have read and written down in the earlier part of this book, list those "body","doing" and "thinking" signs that tell you that you are getting angry.

List below five body signs that let you know that you are becoming angry.

1._____

2._____

3._____

4._____

5._____

List below five doing or action signs that let you know that you are becoming angry.

1._____

2._____

3._____

4._____

5._____

List below five self-talk or thinking signs that let you know that you are becoming angry.

1._____

2._____

3._____

4._____

5._____

In the spaces below, list five situations that tend to make you angry. Try to include situations that occur quite often and to which you usually react to by feeling angry.

1._____

_____

_____

2._____

_____

_____

3._____

_____

_____

4._____

_____

_____

5._____

_____

_____

The staging process

Remember, it always is easier to face anger situations if you take them one step at a time. Break the situation down into four steps. Prepare for teasing and insulting remarks by reminding yourself not to take them personally. During the confronting stage, tell yourself to stay calm and roll with the flow. During the coping with your angry feelings stage, remind yourself that you have a right to be annoyed, but try to contain these feelings for the time being. Lastly, during the thinking back on the "how the whole thing started" stage, be sure to pat yourself on the back if the problem is resolved. If the problem is not worked out, remind yourself that the situation is a difficult one and that it will take some time to straighten out.

Feeling controls

There are two types of feeling controls. One is emotional control for your body: relaxation training. The other is feeling control for your mind: keeping in better humor.

When you stop to think about it, we put a lot of pressure on our bodies every day. We bump them into walls. We make our muscles push huge amounts of weight when we work out. Most of us have anxious or angry feelings that we store in different parts of our bodies. This is troubling because it is not necessary to store angry and anxious feelings in our bodies. We put enough strain on our bodies with our daily routines. We do not need any extra pressure. That extra pressure can actually cause us physical problems, such as headaches. Remember the anger bag that was so full that it was bursting at the seams?

We all store up anger in different places in our bodies. Some of us store anger in our heads and get tension headaches. Others have tension in the neck or upper shoulders. Still others have tightness in their chest or abdomen.

What about you? Do you have any tension in your body? Many times, you may not notice that you are tense. Then, when you sit down in a quiet spot and try to relax, you notice it. You may realize that your muscles are sore or tense. Your arms may hurt. Until you learn how to relax and when to relax, you will stay very tense. You will keep those tensions stored up in different areas of your body.

Remember, you cannot feel relaxed and tense at the same time. That is why we talked about the importance of learning how to relax. It is difficult to have a lot of worries and feel playful at the same time. That is why you have to try to develop a good sense of humor and try to be in a better mood. Life is not all bad. If it were, a person's body and mind would wear out very quickly. You need to have humor in your life to cope with the many problems that occur each day. You need a few good belly laughs. You do not have to take everything seriously.

To start with, there are funny things that happen during the day. Secondly, there are funny things that other people say or do in your school. Try reading a funny book. Watch a comedy on television. Those are just one form of humor. There are also activities that are fun, such as basketball, volleyball, or softball. Through these games, you can take a break from life's heavy problems. The purpose of humor is to provide some distance from the difficult situations that we face every day. Humor helps us keep a balance in our thinking, feelings, and actions.

Besides, people do not like to be around gloomy people. They do not like to spend time with others who have a dark outlook on life. Think about it. Think about how you enjoy hanging around with someone who likes to tell a good joke. You enjoy people who are playful and lively. That does not mean that they totally ignore the serious things in life. It just means that, for the most part, they cope. They make the bad things in life easier to take because they look on the bright side.

Comedy and a sense of humor is something that people always look for today. Consider the movies that come from Hollywood. Top actors make substantial incomes. So do many top comedians. People pay a lot of money to see a stand-up comedy routine. These comedians have the gift of laughter. People spend money to have these comedians help them forget their problems, at least for the moment. Comedians also let us look at our problems from a different point of view. People naturally seem to be attracted to comedians. That is probably because they think that a humorous outlook is worthwhile.

You may never become a big comedian. That is okay! However, remember that you will be way ahead of the game if you just develop a good sense of humor.

Doing or action controls

Doing controls are what we do in a situation when we start to get angry. We touched on doing (or action) controls earlier when we talked about your Anger Logs. We talked about how the outcome of a situation will depend on our nontalking cues. These cues include our body movements and our tone of voice.

To a large extent, your actions are affected by thinking controls such as appraisal, expectation, and self-talk. Your actions are also affected by your feeling controls (relaxation) and your sense of humor. Your thoughts, feelings, and actions are all tied together. Each one affects the others. This means that if you take some steps toward controlling your thoughts and feelings, your actions will be under control.

For example, your thoughts tell you to slow down and take a problem-solving approach. In that situation, you are less likely to act out and kick or punch. In the same way, if your body feels relaxed instead of tense, you are less likely to let the punches fly.

This is especially true if you have developed a sense of humor and are not always bogged down with only the heavy concerns of life.

One of the main things that you have learned from this book is how to make changes. You have learned to develop the behavior you need to deal with problems. You have learned to keep anger from building up inside you. You know that built-up anger only makes a situation worse—worse for yourself and worse for others. Get used to dealing with situations right away, before they get out of hand. Deal with situations while they are just issues. Do not wait until they become confrontations. To do this, make sure your thoughts are on the right track. Make sure your feelings are relaxed. Do not get out your claws! Keep a cool head. Take a problem-solving approach. Do not take things personally. Stick around and find a solution even if it is an "I'll meet you halfway solution."

Afterword

You now have learned what is really meant by the term "anger"—and you have examined your own patterns of anger and found ways to be in charge of yourself and your anger. You have learned about the good and bad uses of anger. You now have a lot of knowledge about angry feelings and situations that you tend to react to by feeling angry.

You have taken a great deal of time to answer questions. You have used much energy making this book worthwhile. By this time, you have made a decision to follow through on some of the ideas presented here. You now know about outside and inside reasons, thinking, feeling, and doing reasons, and the importance of self-talk. You have decided to try to get a handle on your angry feelings.

Ask yourself these questions: Did you think you would make it all the way through this book? How does it feel now that you have done it? Do you look at yourself, others, and at situations differently now? You should. That is what this book is all about. It would be hard to believe you have not made some big changes by now.

Maybe it has not "sunk in," yet. Remember, we talked about walking around with your puppet strings hanging out—just waiting for someone else to control you? If you walk around with your strings hanging out, there always will be others around who are ready and willing to try to make you angry.

Situations may happen where others are quite open about pulling your strings. They may say, "Hey, you stunk on the basketball court yesterday!" Or they may be more subtle. However, things will be different for you—now. By reading this book and answering the questions, you have taken much more control of your life. You have put those puppet strings inside where they belong, or better yet, you have snipped them off. You now have a tool kit for taking care of yourself. You now have the knowledge and skills you need to handle anger situations. You now know the importance of self-talk. You know the importance of relaxation. Additionally, you are armed with specific things to do and say when you are faced with anger situations.

In short, you are more prepared for the challenges of living in today's world than you have ever been before. Now that you have learned to control your anger, a large roadblock has been removed. No longer will "anger" interfere with your plans.

What you have just gone through is not that common. Most people have not had the chance to read a book like this one, or they have not felt that they needed it. Yet, you have done it, and you are much further ahead.

Now that you have learned some skills that may help you to manage your anger, do not lose them! It took a lot of time and hard work for you to learn them. Nevertheless, all that effort can be wasted if you do not practice these skills. Keep these skills in the front part of your mind (the active part). Remember that old expression, "use it or lose it." You should be practicing your new skills every day. Better yet, you should be living them every day.

What you have learned is important. You have revealed a lot about yourself: the old ways you used to think and the new ways you now think. This book is your journal. You have become its writer. You have written about your feelings, your actions, and your thoughts about anger. By doing that, you have made this book an important part of your life. That makes this book a valuable resource for you. You have taken some very important steps in dealing with your problems. You have worked hard at getting control of your anger. This book has given you a good knowledge base of what to do. In short, this book is your chance, your new lease on life! That is what makes this book so important to you.

Now that you have learned all of these new skills, do not just sit back and get lulled into the false sense that you are on top of any situation that arrives. Situations change.

People change. You might think that you have figured someone out and all of a sudden he starts to act differently. You have to recognize that change and use your new skills to handle him differently.

Finally, you change! You may become more sociable or you may become more of a loner. Physically, you may gain weight and become more muscular. If you did, people would react to you differently in "heated" situations. They may feel more threatened by you. If that happened, you might think about using instrumental aggression (that is where you pretend that you are angry when you really are not, just to get something).

The opposite can be true. You may lose weight and look more like a pushover. That, too, would affect how you interact with others in anger situations. Other people might think they could walk all over you. You now have the skills to treat yourself and others with respect.

Such changes may have an effect on your success rate in these situations. Just remember, be aware of changes in yourself and in others, and adjust the way you relate to people.

Believe it or not, one of the nicest things that you could do for someone else is to talk to them about reading a book such as this one. Many people could benefit from it. You did!

You may be asking, where should I go from here? Consider dealing with some of the issues from your past that are still bothering you. For example, try to sort out problems that you may still have with your family members, friends, or teachers. Consider joining groups such as Alateen or Al-Anon Family Groups to deal with stress from family members who abuse alcohol or drugs. It is not necessary for you to carry those problems around with you anymore.

One last piece of advice. Do not forget your sense of humor and the importance of laughter. Laughter is what saves us from many of the grim aspects of this world. Yes, there is a time for sadness, even for crying. However, sadness and hate have been overused. There is too much of both of them in the world. Do not add to it.

Laughter and a good sense of humor are the best ways to battle sadness and hate. Remember, it is difficult to be in a good mood and sad at the same time. Try to lay back and go with the flow. You will be surprised at how little situations hurt when you feel good about yourself.

You have made a very good start toward feeling good about yourself. Remember, you must practice your new skills if you are to reach your goal of controlling your anger. Start putting those skills to work for you—today. You will discover that a happier and more peaceful world can be yours if you learn to "cage your rage." You have made it this far. You can make it all the way!

Suggested Readings

Many of the concepts presented in this book were first proposed by other authors. If you would like to learn more about controlling your anger, you might want to read some of their books and articles listed here.

Burns, D. 1980. *Feeling good: The new mood therapy*. New York: William Morrow.

Charlesworth, E. A., and R. G. Nathan. 1985. *Stress management: A comprehensive guide to wellness*. New York: Atheneum.

Cullen, M. and R. E. Freeman-Longo. 1995. *Men & anger: A relapse prevention guide to understanding and managing your anger*. Brandon, VT: The Safer Society Press.

Ellis, A. 1973. The no cop-out therapy. *Psychology Today* (July): 56 62.

Goldstein, A. P., and A. Rosenbaum. 1982. *Agress-less: How to turn anger and aggression into positive action*. Englewood Cliffs, N.J.: Prentice-Hall.

McInnis, S. n.d. *Who's in charge here? (A guide to putting anger in its place)*. Fairbanks, Alaska: Lettershops.

Novaco, R. W. 1975. *Anger control: The development and evaluation of an experimental treatment*. Lexington, Mass.: Lexington Books.

_____ 1983. Stress inoculation therapy for anger control. *In Innovations in clinical practice: A source book*, vol. 2, edited by P. A. Keller and L. G. Ritt. Sarasota, Fla.: Professional Resource Exchange.

_____ n.d. *Stress inoculation for anger and impulse control*. Therapist manual prepared for Prevention of Relapse in Sex Offenders. Dr. Richard Laws, Principal Investigator. Sponsored by the National Institute of Mental Health.

Neidhardt, E. J., R. F. Contry, and M. S. Weinstein. 1981. *A guided self-management series for stress-related disorders*. Vancouver, B.C.: Western Center Health Group.

Sonkin, D. J., and M. Durphy. 1982. *Learning to live without violence: A handbook for men.* San Francisco: Volcano Press.

Zillman, D. 1979. *Hostility and aggression.* Hinsdale, N.J.: Lawrence Erlbaum Associates.